Seeking Holy Honesty

99 awkward poems
a bunch of odd pictures
and 3 downside-up songs

Stephen Joseph Wolf

idjc.org

Seeking Holy Honesty
Copyright © 2013
Stephen Joseph Wolf
All rights reserved. No part of this book may be copied or reproduced in any form or by any means, except for the inclusion of brief quotations in a review, without the written permission of the author publisher.

Song texts herein composed by Stephen J. Wolf
Ezekiel Song (page 111) and *Blessed Are* (pages 118-119) are now in the public domain.

The photographers of the poet are mostly unknown; other photographs are by Stephen Joseph Wolf.

Printed in the U.S.A. and distributed by Ingram; published by idjc press; contact steve@idjc.info or visit www.idjc.org.

ISBN 978-1-937081-13-3

idjc press books are available in Nashville at St. Mary's Bookstore www.stmarysbookstore.com, and fine bookstores everywhere.

Seeking Holy Honesty

99 awkward poems, a bunch of odd pictures,
and 3 downside-up songs

Contents

Youth Pix of the Poet	6
Holy Honesty	7
I Am Simon Peter	8
A Storytelling Imagining	9
Visitation	10
Dry Brown Leaf	11
Look At My Hands, My Feet	12
Body In Conflict	13
Get Me A Priest!	14
Homeless Paul	15
We'll Talk To Your Father	16
Ash Wednesday	17
Monte Cassino Walk	18
Breathe and Move	21
College Pix of the Poet	23
Evidence	24
Ed	25
So I Say	26
Abba, Deddy & Me	28
What's So Funny?	30
Brother Sister	31
Expectations	32
Mountains Moving	33
Haiti Beach Rain	34
This Hits	36
Walking The Vocation	37
God's Not Done With Us	38
The Daily Cross	39
And Help Me When I Don't	40
Question For The Future	41
IDJC Promises	42

Zechariah In The Visitation	44
Revelation Dream	45
Jesus Calling	46
Arms Out Still Holding Rosary	47
A Meal Is Messy	48
No King?	49
A Necessity?	50
With You	51
Pattern	52
Cain On Trial	53
Plagues	54
Prayer Of Ease	55
Way To Go	56
Lord Adonai	57
From Disciples Called Some Chosen	58
Everyone In The Crowd	59
Demons To Swine	60
Homeless Thanksgiving	61
Terror Struggles	62
Mary A Priest?	63
A Kid's Lie Remembered	64
Conscience Contribution	65
Behind	66
Outcasts Suitable	67
Shoreline	68
Who Do You Say?	69
Pix of the Poet: Accountant, then Priest	70
Servant at the Last Supper	72
Watching Cows Eating Breakfast	74
Carrots	75
Healthy Unhealthy Laugh	76
An Easter Prayer For Vocations	77
Void Filler	78
Names Of The Lord	79
Blockhead Blocks	80
Kenosis	81
They Will Teach You	82

A Prayer For Catholic Charities	83
Fraud	84
Twelve Years Old	85
Prodigal Son Penance	86
Come, Holy Jesus	88
I Am Doing Something New	89
Bartmaeus, to a Michael Jackson Melody	90
Labyrinth	92
Resurrection Emotions	93
A Take On That Oldest English Poem	94
A Real Desire	95
Investigation	96
September 11 Morning	97
The Children	98
Free Slave	99
Betty the Poet	100
Advent Silence	101
Morning Treasure	102
Gift From Little Grace	103
Poverty Immensity	104
Evolution of a Hike-Breath Prayer	105
Before the Crucifix	106
Last Leaves	107
Christmas Eve	108
A Dream	109
Lord, What You Up To Today?	110
Ezekiel Song	111
Beach Ministry	112
What is Faith?	113
Again Again	114
Miracle Of Now	115
Good Guy	116
Turtle Walk	117
Blessed Are	118
Duck Dunner	120
Night-long Rain	121
A Te Deum Rendering	122

6

Holy Honesty

Lord God, Adonai, Elohim, El Shaddai,
   know my desire to be one with you,
   and help me to know it as well.
You are all mighty, and I am not,
   a human mystery formed thus by you.
You know that sometimes I forget
   and reach for your power-glory.
Why easy to forget you my source?

"In the image of God" you write on one hand;
   "does bad things too" grab-held in the other.
Both words give life, peace, and joy
   when at your call their lift is holy honesty.

Again I wrestle in touch at the gut
   to rest then again in your hands,
in honest freedom discomfort
   op'ning to your presence real,
in your gift of one life alive
   lived now even sometimes grateful,
in the gift of your love dense to the deep.

Lord, know my desire to be one with you,
   and help me to know it as well.

I Am Simon Peter

I am Simon Peter saying: "I am going fishing."
Say with me: "we six will go with you."
A man on the shore tells how to catch fish
and John declares, "It is the Lord;"
a kiss on John's forehead
and a jump to the shore.

We gather for a break-the-fast of bread and fish
that takes its long time wonder:
he takes the bread, the fish, and gives.

Then "Steve, do you love me more than these?"
Around the fire sit the best friends of my life.
I know what is being asked
and tears bust open a grief answer,
a choked out yes.

Bright light over his shoulder, he asks again.
I take my time, for this sob-bed yes to be true.

Out comes the third "yes"
and I *FEEL* the light and am laughing.
So are they,
and so is he.

A Storytelling Imagining

When they are teenagers,
Jesus tries to tell a close friend who he is.

The young man becomes frightened to crying,
pulls himself together, and tells his mother.

Mary hears word of it
and has a long walk and talk
with her newly lonelier son.

Jesus stays in the company of this friend,
as they somewhat keep up their shared guard.

It is this friend into whose eyes Jesus looks
at Cana when he asks Mary the question,
"why a concern to you and to me?"

> His friend's mother had died
> the same year as Joseph
> and at the burials
> becoming again very close
> have not yet had the real discourse
> over their friendship teen sharing.

How do they talk about it now?

Visitation

Elizabeth tells a young neighbor daughter
the story of Mary's visit.
The girl dismisses it all as mutterings
of a dying woman, and finishes
feeding her the food her own mother sent.

After the Saving Dying and Rising
she takes her grown-up food to Mary,
the sad mother who is not sad at all,
and they talk about Elizabeth
and all kinds of things.

Dry Brown Leaf

A great little stroll in the yard
  with a notecard
  and a rusty accountant pencil
  hidden in a jacket pocket chill.
A plain brown leaf is caught in a shoe;
  it is beautiful, held up to the sun:
  how many shades of brown can there be?
Beauty is in the light shining through it
  into me.

On the west side of the front yard
  a large tree has been cut to a stump.
The spiral center point is a bit off geographic.
It took three saw cuts to get at the center,
  angled all slightly down.
When I step up and onto the stump
  a piece breaks off
  in the shape of a dry brown leaf.

Look At My Hands, My Feet

I kneel at the feet of Jesus
  and hold his left hand in my own.
Thumbs explore inside his palm,
  rough, strong, beaten, whole…
Face buries in his cloak
  and he holds my face in this hand.
Lean your rest into him;
  he holds the neckback
  in his warm right hand,
  as he speaks to the others.
And I hear every word.

Body In Conflict

Stepping into the cool rectory
after a long hot summer run
(ok, let's call it a jog),
the pastor Fleming seeing sweat dripping
declares "do you think this is wise?"
    I have no answer.
Next morning seeing my fatman breakfast
he offers "you really are a body in conflict!"
    My response is not altogether necessary:
     "This coming from a man
       who eats ice cream for breakfast?"
His pleased face disappears
behind the sports page.
He is right; I am a body in conflict;
and why does it feel
like this is how it is supposed to be?

Get Me A Priest!

"Get me a priest!" she tells them!
Mid-forties, away from home, alone,
in real pain, pins and braces on both legs,
neck sewn up, she has to be very still,
and they come in and tell her they are
taking her down for some procedures.
She freaks out, "Get me a priest!"
"Through
this holy anointing…"
she becomes
very calm.

Homeless Paul

Paul sits in the center row, end of the pew.
Good people shift in their seats
and no one is sitting anywhere near him.

The smell yesterday was as strong as ever,
the worst of it from that nasty blanketcoat.

Then, during the commotion of the collection
a young man (a Vanderbilt student?)
goes across the aisle and sits next to Paul
and stays there the rest of the mass.

> Five minutes with him yesterday
> in the one little room of reconciliation,
> and I wanted to beg for mercy.

This young man is . . . what?
a living saint?
in a conversion experience?
totally lacking in sense of smell?
This I know:
I am touched and edified.

We'll Talk To Your Father

A little girl is to be baptized.
Me: Will her father be here?
Mother: He is incarcerated.
I make a bad joke about the Catholic thing
and the little girl's cousin turns to leave.
Age ten or so, he has not yet been baptized.
I grab him and keep a hand on his shoulder
and on his cousin's shoulder,
making eye contact with them both,
attempting assurances of belonging.
He is holding my hand as they leave.
"Momma, I want to be baptized."
"We'll talk to your father."

Ash Wednesday

The deacon thinks 3,000 came through the day.
In the middle of ashing,
   "Remember you are dust
     and to dust you will return"
so many times,
this intimate human crossrub on the forehead,
right hand accepted on the
uncountable shapes of human foreheads
of old friends, new friends, and strangers,
like when anointing the dying,
you get close to a child of God real fast.

Monte Cassino Walk

Past the shrine, down a one-lane gravel road,
past rolled bales of sweet smelling hay,
past a pond next to a barn,
to an open flat field of grass
on top of this grand hill,
nobody but me and a lot of bugs.
A white carload of teenagers
parks under a tree for a while, but leaves.
I ask the question I've been asking,
"Lord, how do you know me?"
    "I love you."
"But when you love me, what do you know?"
    Nothing;   nada;   no thing accused.
Then bursts forth from somewhere deep:
"I know, Lord God that you love me.
 Not faithful in prayer, not present to people,
 ungiving to the poor, not there for the sick,
 not eager to serve…where's the love?
 Lord, I accuse myself of failing to do love."
Sitting on this road
shooing flies with the shirt off my back
watching bees visit clover
and butterflies caring for the pasture,

sitting, I barely see over the grass,
and what I see is warm beauty.
Trees line the edges of this flat hilltop.
A still tractor is parked in the distance.
Clouds make things cool and interesting,
and clouds moving bring back the sun,
and again it feels just plain good.
Do horseflies enjoy this swatting game?
Standing up renews awares
of an earlier noticed symbol of faith.
The one-lane drive tees out in a cross,
to one side manure/mulch/compost piles;
> the first pile does not smell sweet,
> and I check no further.

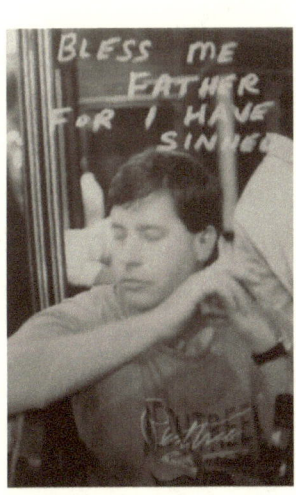

The other "arm" of the T cross is just
>more one-lane drive going to nowhere
without end but seeming to fade out
as it enters the warm beauty
of the side of the field
on that big flat hilltop.

I see the neatly stored sin of my failures
on one side,
and an opening to all that is good and beautiful
and loving on the other.
Both sides are real; the field is not divided.
Butterflies and horseflies and bees are all over.
Walking away, saying again,
"I have not been loving God or neighbor,"
I stop,
turn around,
and face the T cross:
>"I have not been loving you…
> but you have not stopped loving me."

I raise my arms, for a good while yet,
and offer a prayer
of thanks and praise and love.
And I come down off of that hill, different.
Yes, Lord, you know everything.
You know well that I love you.

Breathe and Move

Is it wind in trees or rain on grass?
Even the good ear tunes not that sharp.

But if window is open and if heart is clear
and if soul is still and one lung moves air

Then drying wind is felt on skin
or wetting rain is felt in bone.

May it be safe to breathe a breeze
yet too much rain might wet too wet.

So with window propped
    and since heart is clear
a soul still blessed with lungs that fill

I do have faith to leave the room
move bones in rain and breathe in wind.

22

A Geyser in Iceland

Gullfoss

Arles

Charlie & Jeanette Wolf, the 25th Wedding Anniversary, with
Danny, Steve, Pat, Greg, David, Andrew, Kevin & Matthew

Evidence

real bread fish and oil   wine to warm the heart
water used to drink and clean
                         and call us to new art

lipitor prozac hot   coffee and iced coke
all of it seems legal so
                         laugh at the next good joke

good job ordinary wage   work I wish I had
except the one who's got it
                         looks like he's been had

blue chip poker wager   money in the bank
something to retire on
                         and helpers to be frank

girl friend boy friend
                         friends who don't have sex
thank God for the good friend
                         who helps keep me in check

fishing pole radio tube   books and other gifts
thank you Lord for who you are
                         and evidence of this

Ed

the shock was near too much to bear
a best friend of our fathers shot
struggling for life in a room in a hospital
named for a saint of great doubt
some brothers gather at home like so many
bells ring, the oldest hangs up: he is dead.
good people bear pall on the third day
of "how can this be," and at the packed house
some fellow standing no named hand
rubs into one shoulder some peace.

So I Say

They said it was the cancer
in breast then lung then head
she fought back and back and then
voice inverse limbs in seize til still
no, this strong Mary laughing loud
    absorbed pain to her limit
    trusting and hoping for better and full
    for all around who she tempered it from
- so I say, she still laughs out loud.

They said it was his drinking
drugs and deals and beer too much
I wish I'd known him closer
in some grown up time to share
no, maybe our time was plenty good
    jokes and torturing sisters
    bikes baseball brothers and smokes
    charged with passion of cousins who can
- so I say, he still knew the way home.

They said it was her bad luck
wrecks and falls and one bad burn
laughing gas too loose or stuck
(anesthesia is risk, whoever does the turn)

no, humor she had and did not speak ill
    so good she was she did not see
    we wish her pain had spoken plain
    her friends desired to cross that sea
 - so I say, she still trusts her travel.

They said it was the smoking
bringing both early death
but eighty four and eighty
are good terms for the strong
no, cigarettes did cost them
    boxes of voice that work so those
    last years they sounded the same
    as the same machines that talk
 - but I say, they could still kiss.

They said it was a bad heart
in this best man I've known
a heart for two wives and lives
sons and daughters by law and grands
no, this champion heart of gentle good
    strong with hand and smart with tool
    could only be loved so much until
    a fullness burst and boat to shore
 - so I say, he still whistles his chuckle.

Abba, Deddy & Me

I'm glad to have told to hey deddy
the things that most weighed me down
a telling the toughest of all
the honesty gifts free to free

our words and our hugs became true
sacred ritual sacred as Sunday kept
Mayberry and Braves in our good thoughts
spoke now the way best friends do

there was a day later he dropped
in my lap his best radio journal
pointed his surety "you'll like this"
two hobby dads, one same story

when small and he grown were going
the way he would tie up my shoe
was lean in and reach all around me front
well shod and warm I might be

when his fight was done with no shame
the game he had lost he had won
we gathered around to honor in honesty
good love good work and the heard

now I've heard lots of folk tell their story
so know how it is to hear truth
it rarely is easy most often rewards
when the telling loops into God's ear

this grateful son told to hey deddy
of weight not light deaf or dumb with
warts bumps bruises and lumps it's usually
best when one loved hears the hum

What's So Funny?

sit down I choose a chair toward some mountains
in this corner view their highnesses blocked
by yet growing bushes scrub oak on cliff edge
watch! these little leaves dance in the air
and tug at the twigs holding onto them there,
what breaks without grip into one laughing ball?
me. it's just too hilarious.

Brother Sister

the little brother loved the bazaar
last Sunday, a first time to church,
his sad question cried "where's the bazaar?"
when we left started home it hit, oh no,
momma said, to herself she wished,
what error to bring him last week
wanting worship to mean for him fun
how can it ever be that fun again,
strange the cycle, though, no danger done
he's grown; they take both of their sons.

it was my job to make bad news public
move close to the door, brace for riot
first a warning of tragedy coming
remember, we are community, so hear
the bad news: no donuts this week.
we know not why, rarely horror makes sense,
in difficult times hear our call:
can we be there for each other?
small girl empties tears into preacher, is asked
do you forgive, will you come back? yes. yes.

Expectations

I DO NOT EXPECT THE CHURCH
TO BE PERFECT,
NOR DO I WANT "OUTSIDERS"
POINTING OUT IMPERFECTIONS.
BUT WHO BETTER FOR THAT THAN
A SELF-PROCLAIMED OUTSIDER?
NO, THAT'S NOT IT,
BECAUSE IF I BELIEVE WHAT I SAY
I BELIEVE ABOUT "CHURCH"
THEN NO ONE IS AN OUTSIDER.
WILL WE EVER STOP TRYING
TO PROVE THE CONTRARY?
And so the crux and the cross:
MY SINFUL DESIRE
TO BE PROUD OF MY CHURCH.

Mountains Moving

The mountains they move Haiti-slow
call through to the source that is
deep both beyond and behind
wave high common heart to the high.

Oh sure, my head knows they don't dance
except in illusion of light
shadows of shrink and growth matched
to desire for shared life, that thing more.

Some places are with no real mountains
concrete, glass, steel, pieced with wood
deceiving "it's better than hills,
above dirty earth so, therefore better."

Yeah, clean things move if not well
hard shiny smooth silent still
too much to say clean has died
when in sterile breeze seem to have.

So let these mountains make wave
in a haze of mix, cloud sun and wind
let us watch even deep away far:
Move mountains! Call a dance deep to high!

Haiti Beach Rain

Some rain not all people see
this could not be some something else
not a spray, by no measure drizzle
wet falling, source up, so what else?

But we in the water could see it
hot toasting sun singing through it
hands held over heads in eye shade
can dance with the sun bounced off rain.

Admit we the sprinkle was so soft
more than mist, sure, not quite drizzle
its hit on the hand had no sting
to take offense or draw a defense.

But beauties bathing we try to collect
into pleasant pools cupped in palm skin
even our countless nerves of four human hands
not nerve enough, endings too soon.

Our friends on their own dry land shore
in tree shade with backs to the star
saw not this warm wet light vision
saw four of each: raised arm and palm.

So we in the water were asking
the question that good friends might pose
are we crazy? or why can't they see it?
since two or more give valid witness.

When Adonai greets people "good day!"
the gift might be place and position
thanksgiving poised to see and to hear
one dance of some rain in light real.

This Hits

Too much work,
too much to do,
prayer is a solace,
but exercise bites.
This hits:

> Even if, in my weakness,
> judged by the Judge *negative!*
> and due to my fault alone,
> even if cut off always,
> God will still love me!

Even if in hell to eternity,
while then and there,
God would still be loving me.
May be the hell of it
would be the not knowing it,
but God would still be loving me.
And the knowing of this is the real freedom.

Walking the Vocation

breeze, sun warmth, cows, trees, vine,
broken tree limb, sound of leaves,
an unusual fragrance sweet,
a smell like a bad sneeze,
spicy taste from lunch,
stagnant water, two men talking in a barn,
gravel crunching underfoot,
my own heavy breathing, a raven(?) flying off

A sun's steady movement through the day
knows its own course
giving generously without losing itself?
    Is it not giving up its lifespan too?
    Is it not dying very slowly also?
Is not all creation called to these? me too?

Lord, keep me faithful, keep me willing,
       keep refreshing,
       keep growing me in wisdom and grace,
       keep me joyful, and
       keep my eyes open.
Lord, keep me varied and balanced,
       keep me from losing hope,
       keep me.

God's Not Done With Us
Meditation on Isaiah 45:7-13

"Steve, making well-being, I allow woe."
    Yes, Lord, you have made me well and low.
"Steve, dare the clay question its modeler?"
    Lord, yes, I have dared so to say:
        Is this as good as you do?
    Indeed peculiarities awareness
        is enough to retreat and to like them;
        been told how particular I can be.
    What I need, no, beg, ask of my molder:
        What would you have me like fairly?
        What too should I know as low woe?
    And then dare make the ask for some water
        for soft'ning of clay hard'ning fast;
    because God, our God, is not done yet
        with any of us, of certain, not yet.

The Daily Cross

Onto
the breast daily
a cross on a string
what a facile
thing
compared to
what he did.
And yet
this little sign
I make,
and remember
that I
have been taken
possession of
by Christ.

And Help Me When I Don't

I roam the house sitting
before crucifix after crucifix.
The most haunting is the white porcelain cross,
breakable, in the St. Alphonse chapel.
The Lord is gaunt,
weak memory of strength,
hands given to bent fingers,
head slumped almost into armpit,
legs loose,
knees dangling out
as if swinging in a violent wind.
Lord Jesus Christ,
Son of the Living God,
have mercy on me
a sinner,
THE sinner,
since you would have done this
for only me.
Some first-time confessors know this.
Help me to love you
enough to always say Yes!
(And help me when I don't.)

Question For The Future

A question for the future:
Which will see victory? Workaholism?
                                            Laziness?

Probably neither or both;
   be honest about the connections.

Yes.

My undisciplined laziness
   lets me say a now and then yes
   to the workahol druggy addiction.

A balanced life:
does it not allow for a more complete response
   to the Lord's call to mission? Still,
   my presence in the real presence
   to others who are sick
   will be the real prediction story.

Thank you, Lord, for your loving patience!

IDJC Promises
(Integrating Disciple of Jesus Christ)

I promise as a lifegiver priest
    for Jesus our Savior
to be in communion in the Sunday assembly,
    day by day in my family, the domestic Church,
    as a bearer of the mystery of Christ,
to be known by God in private prayer,
    honest confession, and maturing hope,
to forgive from the heart and accept forgiveness,
    and so spread the healing presence of Christ.

I promise as a soldier prophet
    confirmed in faith by the Holy Spirit seal
to put on the mind of Christ,
    learning the inspired text
    and dealing first with the violence in me,
to honor Jesus as teacher, model, goal,
    and King of kings,
    and speak his truth with compassion,
to be on mission to reveal his face on all people,
    especially on the wounded and marginalized,
    and so give witness to his brand of peace.

I promise as a footwasher royal
    for God my Father
to name the gifts of my birth and baptism
    and tend to their growth,

to accept responsibility for what I do,
to participate in God's ongoing creation
    giving generously of time, talent and treasure,
    and so serve as one builder of gospel justice.

I promise as a beloved lover
    of our loving God
to honor my role as child, (parent,) sibling,
    and friend, seeking to be known by risking trust
    in vital relationships with a few others,
to grow in gratitude, integrity, humility and
    patient charity,
to respect all women and men in equality,
    and remain faithful
    to my vocation to love and be loved,
    and so be one living sign
        of the renewal of God's covenant.

Lord, Jesus Christ, Son of the Living God,
I am _____, your baptized follower, seeking
    the mercy, justice, fidelity and knowledge of God
    that the Father seeks and to which you lead.
Send your Holy Spirit; help me to be faithful
    to the will of our Father and to your call
    and so abide in love with you.
Have mercy on me,
    your disciple, servant, sibling and friend.
Amen.

Zechariah In The Visitation

Elizabeth is filled 6/9 with John Baptizer,
                 9/9 with the Holy Spirit;
Mary too, the two, women-joy shatter-exploding.
Zechariah, silenced, sticks around the house,
       loves it all, but rolls a lot his eyes
       and shakes a lot his head.
After a long time of quiet as the women work
       comes a long and slow building laughter
       that leaks into the uncontrollable.
Zechariah smiles a polite, but has to take a walk;
       it's just too much joy to take.

It's raining now. I (Zechariah) am forced to stay in.
The women have seen me roll my eyes,
so they try to keep it under control.
It will not be kept, and trying makes it worse.
They are pounding the table they laugh so hard
       then a slow quiet down.
I monk-sign, "perhaps a nap?"
Their nods look down, trying to be sober.
False sobriety becomes too much even for me;
a walk over to the table and a silent-mouthing
of the last word that had set them off laughing,
and off go the three of us, pounding the table,
with John kicking it and the Trinity singing,
"Not since Isaac has there been such joy!"

Revelation Dream

an old friend from youth courts me lavishes
many small but heartfelt gifts onto me
a love true and mine still is
as all feels very good and at some level
very right though wonder why
this did not happen earlier but know
of my too great fear as we look at each other
and smile for the longest time knowing
the love we have for each other means
this could be perfect and good but
before the dream is over have had to say
no to this courting while our love would go on
there is a greater fuller richer complete and
true love to which my freely given yes must go
and freely do say yes and there is
this friend's loving and understanding smile
that knows our love will not end and yet sees
my beatitude of being what they call
soulmate
in Christ

Jesus Calling

Jesus knows my questions
Jesus is a welcoming host
Jesus gives me a new name
Jesus knows what it is to be called
Jesus uses us to find each other
Jesus sees our deepest resting places
Jesus knows his own mysterious name
Jesus cures to enable hospitality
Jesus heals to get us ready to hear him
Jesus knows his purpose
Jesus knows what it is to be sent
Jesus comes to where we live
Jesus knows where the fish are
Jesus lifts me up to his purpose
Jesus takes away my fear
Jesus knows my name

Lord Jesus, you know where I am
    and you know
        I like being caught by you.

Arms Out Still Holding Rosary

Father, I thank you
Father, I praise you
Father, I believe in you
Father, I hope in you
Father, I love you.

>Jesus, I thank you
>Jesus, I praise you
>Jesus, I believe in you
>Jesus, I hope in you
>Jesus, I love you.

>>Spirit, I thank you
>>Spirit, I praise you
>>Spirit, I believe in you
>>Spirit, I hope in you
>>Spirit, I love you.

>Thank you, God, for loving me.
>TYGFLM

A Meal Is Messy

A meal is messy A meal is necessary A meal is life-giving A meal is a blessing A meal is ritual A meal is a place to laugh and cry A meal keeps my mouth busy A meal lets me listen A meal takes time A meal has to be cooked A meal has to be cleaned up A meal makes content the beast A meal opens the mind A meal swells the heart A meal strengthens the body A meal leads to a nap A meal brings up memories A meal creates new memories A meal has an end.

And then we become hungry again.

25th birthday peach cobbler

No King?

The Chief Priests said out loud
those scandal-words most sad in all the bible:
>   We have no king but Caesar.

In giving them every chance
to let him let go the Christ
Pilate cornered them
into forgetting their God.

This is how the subtle system works,
is it not?

No king, and God there and everywhere!
Heartbreak coldness matches
the cold prison night of our Lord.

> Jesus, I am sorry
> for all the ways
> that night was cold
> and for all the ways
> this night is cold
> for you in
> your brothers and sisters,
> my sisters and brothers.

A Necessity?

This was not necessary ! ! !
Why couldn't they just let him keep teaching?
Because they would have had to change;
we would all have had to change.
Maybe, I suppose, I guess, maybe my God
this *was* necessary ! ! !

With You

I want to kneel
in the empty tomb
with hand-palms flat
on the cool hewn stone shelf
and praise God
for what happened here.

Is this the source
of my hands palm-flat
reverence-linger at the altar?

But there I cannot stay
too called
to be sent:
Can I not now say?
I have met the Lord
who has said to me:
I am
the one
who has been
with you
every moment
of every day
and every night.

Pattern

In the night, lightning without rain
and a shooting star and my restless heart.
Standing before the high window naked
arms raise in thanks, praise, belief, hope, love,
breathing in the breath of life, exhaling
sorrow over the suffocation of the Savior
now breathing on us all
the living grace
and saying,

> Do not worry about anything except this:
> You, you Steve, you follow me.

The new seamless garment
moves in the risen form
and my walk is one step and then the other
behind
his whole new way
of being and relating:

> Seeing this pattern of your robe
> alive again is the I that I am.

Cain On Trial

Bob watched on the History Channel
about Cain and Abel and is impressed
with how God sought to protect Cain
with a mark
that no human may hurt him,
God's court of law after the first murder.

(When I praise God for wisdom genius
 I hear a bemused thank you,
 as if God needs my encouragement!)

Bob is grateful for how God kept
coming after him on the death penalty.
He is grateful for conversion; imagine
Bob sitting in front of the TV
with his Youth Bible in his lap
and his mind open to God's ways.

Plagues

I read, Lord Jesus,
in 1st Samuel
of the plagues
of hemorrhoids
and mice
and laugh
to the divine sense of humor,
and remembering
the priest gone to glory
who knew and now knows
that God has a sense of humor
and who lived and now lives
in hope and now knowledge
that God judges his jokes
as funny,
think surely this was unfunny
to the people, but surely, Jesus,
you laughed
when you first understood it,
a prelude to your pain
in compass empathy.

Prayer Of Ease

Seminary seedbed prayer of ease
seems lonngg farr awayy,
grace trust in the hands of seminary people.
So help me this day to know
my whole being placed by my whole being
in you
your hands the dwelling constant and near
and keep me there.
TYGFLM.

Way To Go

Lord, take me as you find me
but find me;
bless me as you desire
but bless me;
break me as you know best
but break me;
give me to whom you will
but give me.

Lord Adonai

Lord Adonai, your Son Beloved
calls me beloved brother
asking me to call you Father.
Descendent of your son Adam and
brother of your Son Jesus,
boldly today I claim my birthright.
    Take me as I am,
    Bless me as your son,
    Break me of my sin, and
    Give me back to sons and daughters
        as you see fit.
Amen, amen, amen, amen.

From Disciples Called Some Chosen

How did the unchosen disciples take it?
Still called a disciple, perhaps relieved
safe in the crowd.
I would not have taken it well.

Rejection: insecure pride takes offense.
Being human, feelings hurt, and I am
the little boy whiney-butt
when food is brought in
at Grandmother Gregory's house
for grown-ups who have not yet eaten.
An embarrassment to the Momma,
you'd think the kid had not been fed.
You'd think I was not loved!
The loud pout left a scar on her
leaving also a little boy memory scab.
Goodness sakes.

Remind unhealed vulnerable weakness
that I am loved completely by You!
And am fed from your abundance
with everything I need, and then some.
It is enough.

Everyone In The Crowd
Luke 6:19

We all want to touch you, Lord,
but it is a great crowd!

So you raise your eyes in this level plain,
you touch us with your eyes
and you touch us with your teaching.

Word of God, fill me up!

Demons To Swine

Demon intercession and demons to swine
    (a quick memory: the doctor
      shows where he wrote on my chart:
*patient describes a sense of being
possessed by some kind of demon
compelling him to eat.*)
and people of a town are seized with **fear**.
Fear of what? Worried about the effect possible
that Jesus would have on them?
Had they grown used to their demons?
Did they like knowing where the demons were
  (out of the way outside the town?
   If they're in that guy then they're not in me!)
Are they afraid of the Jesus power?
Am I?
  Lord Jesus,
  if my demon(s) can bargain with you surely
  so can I(?)
  With me in your command,
  let me face my demon(s);
  let me accept where and how you send them;
  and bring me to sit at your feet.
At your feet.

Homeless Thanksgiving

Out of town on Thanksgiving Day
ate at a Methodist Church like a homeless man.
Ate too much, like always…
Reconciling the checking account
caught up on (and in) contributions and bills,
grateful for a grateful heart.

> Lord,
> watch over those
> who could not eat too much today
> and those who have bills to pay
> and troubles on the way.
> Thank you, God of us all,
> for loving us all.

DO NOT BLOCK DOOR

Terror Struggles

Blameless until evil
spreading in far-flung trade
violence becomes our business, and we sin...
haughty of heart because of our beauty...
for the sake of splendor we debase wisdom...
(Ezekiel 28:15-17)

Lord, is this a partial picture
of our U S of A terror struggles?
Does far-flung trade have to be
in the company of violence?
Can we not have both splendor and wisdom?
Is wisdom here the core call?
Amen, it's your ask that we seek wisdom first.
Are you asking us to be all we can be,
> the splendid splendor, so long
> as we do not violate wisdom?

Lord God,
you indeed call us to be queens and kings,
servant kings and queens of the King of kings;
prod us with your Wisdom Word to do,
prod us, move us, prompt us,
> provoke us, poke us, point us,

prod us to ask for her again: Sophia
> Lady Wisdom.

Mary A Priest?

Some beautifully telling feedback
from small groups sharing their faith
has been the good number of women
with honest difficulty
seeing themselves as priests.
> Remember, each
> baptized follower of Jesus Christ
> is a priest, prophet, royal, and lover.
> My nicknames: lifegiver priest
>   soldier prophet
>   footwasher royal
>   beloved lover.

What interests me
in this difficulting is that indeed indeed
some of these baptismal marks, if I may,
would tend to be more classically masculine.
"Priest" is one of those that strikes me
(anyway) as more feminine.
Realizing this scares many of us to the death,
> someone thinking right now,
> "has that boy lost his mind?"

Without going into wholly unholy discourse,
just look at the fervent devotion of Mary.

A Kid's Lie Remembered

Still don't know why I told that lie;
kinda just happened
and to a Sister; lying to a Sister.
"Operation?" She looked at my side.
"I don't see a wound or even a scar.
 You are healed!"
She would give me a smile
or a silent nun fingershake
or a wink to say:
You're ok. Tell the truth. You're ok.

So comes a new thing in prayer
is not a kick; it's an old thing new,
personal vocation deepening:
holy honesty, humble fidelity, so
     honest   fidelity.

Conscience Contribution

Yep; it was in the papers and it's even true;
gave my own maximum money to a politician,
war frustration resulting in catholic hate mail:
such things to say to a priest having a bad day.

What is keeping me from loving God
with all my beater, brain, body & being?
    Feels like the missing of a lost friend.
    Fear about this political thing
        is tied up in fear over being rejected
        not by people who do not know me
        but by people who do.

Lord, the key
is to know what I know:
    You know everything about me!
    And knowing all that!
    You love me!

This is all the acceptance I need.
Why is it not all the acceptance I need?
This is all the acceptance I need.

And still comes the crazy catholic hate mail.

Behind

Lord Jesus, my sins are ever before me
and when weak arrogance sins even again
you remake worth by your mercy.
I say I want to see you, face to face,
but hesitate to ask,
the question of being ready.
I can say and do ask
that I may stand behind you
and kiss your feet.
Grace me with strength to be this weak
and ready me to ask to gaze on
your face, eyes wide open on us all.

Drawing by Grace

Outcasts Suitable

Lord, history says always will be
outcasts suitable for the grumbling
of those enslaved in believing
you came only for them.

As you set free the outcasts
of their rejection shackles
set free too the grumblers;
welcome all us outcast grumblers
and eat with us again.

Shoreline

Lord, all you had to do was be you
and walk the shoreline
and call
and four brothers left their lifework on water
    for the new dryland journey.

How long did it take them
to fully embrace your call
and say "I want to be his apostle"?

There stand the four in front of my hesitation:
    Simon: "Don't worry"
    Andrew: "He is the One"
    James: "Trust him"
    John: "He will be with you"

Who Do You Say?

Steve, who do You say that I am?
You are the One who has been with me
every moment of every day and night.
You did not reject me;
you have not abandoned me.
You are the One God, living me into
the fullness of the covenant
by your fidelity to it.
You are every hope beyond every thing.

You have taken away my shame. Again.

An often wondering: something I did?
Did this growing up thing wrong?
Old Times and New Times answer
a questioning ridiculous.
In your gratitude for my faithful desire,
Lord, you have taken away the shame
you never wanted to be there.

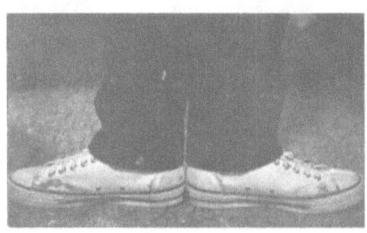

MTSU Grad

14 tax seasons, most with Eric, Charles and Lucy

Hey Deddy and the Boys

about to be ordained a deacon

photo by parishioner Anne
in her sense of humor

newly baptized Christian
named Christian

little brother James, big brother Steve

Servant at the Last Supper

John 13

Lord, I am the servant.
This is my job and it is embarrassing
because I did a job not good enough.
In my hurry;
there is still dirt on their feet.

So still serving am I,
an altar boy on Holy Thursday,
helping with basin and towel.
You know the inadequacy on my mind
and smile the way friends do
and assure me with thanks for helping
but that this is not about me.

When you finish with the twelve
you set the basin before me
and taking my feet, one at a time,
wash them completely clean.
Your teaching is a rubbing
of word into feet.

This has never happened before.
I don't hear a word of your teaching,
though I see you talking, them listening,
and John taking it in with good memory.
I trust he'll fill me in later,
but do hear the words I carry always:

> If you understand this,
> blessed are you if you do it.

Holding
the new-clean foot of your servant
you stop talking
and enter my eyes
and our tears flow.

You call me messenger.

Watching Cows Eating Breakfast

If you ever feel ridiculous
take a good look at some cows
and imagine how ridiculous
they must sometimes feel.
Moo.

Lord, when I began laughing,
had to begin walking away
out of respect for your creative work.

Thank you for taking
this apple kind of delight
in my weirdness ways.

W.C Fields

Carrots

Standing in line for monastery supper
think I see grilled wieners
and saliva makes a move in the mouth.
Is that kraut too? Nope
just noodles and cheese; still good.
Eating these anti-usual dawgs
the brain deciphers: roasted carrots!
mushrooms, onions, olive oil, some spice?,
and the still meaty carrotness.
Gotta try this at home.
So what has my attention
while Nashville is bishopless
and the Cosmos is popeless?
Carrots.
The Station of the Cross shows
Jesus "falling" the first time;
on his way down hands and forearms
in the air to brace the fall.
Do know
what skinned hands look like
and feel like.
Pitiful little has my real suffering been.
Carrots.

Healthy Unhealthy Laugh

May '05 reading sad news
of Boston parishes closing,
a statistic confrontation:
one in three Boston pastors
are over the age of 70.
A laugh begins
that will not stop
alone in the house
a laughing keeps on
it hurts my side
going on and on.
When finally done
so able to stop
and check the clock:
a laugh out of control
for ten solid minutes
feeling not healthy at all
but like something
that needed to come out
did.

An Easter Prayer for Vocations

Come, Holy Spirit,
    fill the hearts of your faithful;
    confirm in us the fire of your love.
Give us wisdom to seek the face of God,
    understanding of our baptism in Christ,
    and right judgment to discern his call
        in freedom.
Give us courage to say yes to our vocations,
    knowledge of what Jesus teaches,
    and reverence for the ways of the Father.
Give us wonder and awe in your presence
    that the witness we give
        to the resurrection of the Son
    may be pleasing to the Father
    and help you, Holy Spirit,
        renew the face of the earth.
Amen.

Void Filler

Reflecting, Lord, on treasuring delights
and your wise designs
this mind of mine floats off
to a contrast of similarity.

When a job is well done
by just about anyone
my interest in interfering is
none.

When the job to be done has gone undone
with no volunteer on horizon
can't do anything but to it
run.

Convinced this stuff comes from you,
wondering whether wonders if it comes from
this weird nature desire that is mine to fill
voids.

Somewhere in the depth
is awe of you and your way;
help me in finding it, Lord,
to live it.

Names Of The Lord

My names, Lord, for you
are names I try to use
for myself:
> lifegiver priest
> soldier prophet
> footwasher king
> beloved lover.

Remember me to remember
the names I try
to let you grow me
are first of all
names for you, Lord.

TYGFLM

Blockhead Blocks

I confess again my idolatry,
my little "g" gods,
named as efforts to be
liked admired thought well of…
Absurd! this sin,
in cognition you alone, Lord,
are the only One
who loves perfectly me.
When will this understanding be final?
All about you,
I confess my sin-tending desire
to stay full of my own spirit.
Help me breathe out the gunk
so to breathe in the Spirit of You.

Kenosis
keh-'noh-sis

It's a Greek word
that's supposed to mean
something like
"self-emptying."

A friend asks about it
after exercise,
then a try to explain
in English words known.

The explanation failing
is not attempted again,
not from fear of a failure repeat
but from the smell of impossibility.

It seems now kenosis mostly happens
on the toilet; this is for sure:
Lord, I cannot do it myself; Help!
Empty me that you may fill me up.

They Will Teach You

Jesus says to them and to all:
"Many things to say…
  but you cannot bear them now…"

> Lord, speak what I can bear;
> your free slave servant is listening.

>> Eyeglasses come off
>> to see what can be seen and
>> blurry eyes see in the trees
>> the outline
>> of a dying man's gasp.

"They will teach you
  what I need you to know."

> Fearing that might be too much(?):
> a hesitant "anything else?"

>> Still waiting in anticipation
>> of surprise. That is to say,
>> still listening.

TYGFLM

A Prayer For Catholic Charities

God, our Father,
> your ways are perfect and true;
> so many of our ways are not.

You give us each
> mind and heart and soul and strength
> to love and serve you in each other.

Our systems, which we construct,
> still leave people hungry and underfed,
> homeless and undereducated,
> unemployed and underemployed,
> uninsured and underinsured,
> abandoned and left on the margins.

Give us, first, Lord,
> the wisdom we need from you
> to build a society more just and peaceful,
> allowing each human being
> the fruits of your creation
> due to him or her in dignity.

And, in the meantime, Lord,
> guide us as people of charity
> who help pick up the pieces
> of a broken world.

Bless our lives
> and all we serve in your name. Amen.

Fraud

I confess, Lord, what we know: I am a fraud.
I can talk all day long about you, about prayer,
    about fidelity, vocation and gratitude.
Yet time I want to spend with you
    is wasted elsewhere,
  prayer I want to be in with you
    is frittered away on nothing,
  fidelity I have promised to you
    is focused on co-creatures,
  my vocation I wear like an absurd cassock,
    a plaything,
  and can't name a thing worthy of gratitude
    except, yes,

I am grateful for you,
who have called me and keep calling me, you,
who stay faithful even when I am not, you,
who keep reminding and remaking me, you,
who love me still.
Yes, Lord, I love you too.

TYGFLM

Twelve Years Old

I am twelve years old.
Jesus and a big crowd are walking
toward town on Broadway, from 20th to 17th.
I go get this sick homeless woman
and finally convince her to go see Jesus.
When she sees him,
we both go up and touch him.
Both of us (with everyone else) deny the touch.
She comes forward on her knees, trembling.
I go to her left arm.
Jesus reaching down
touches her right shoulder
wrapping his arm around hers,
does the same with his right arm
around my left shoulder and arm.
We both pull her up.
Jesus looks at me and recognizes me
as having brought others to him.
Everything in the background freezes in
slow motion, and we're looking at each other
for a long time.

    Prayed the passage again (Luke 8:43-48)
    and all the same, except now fifty.

Prodigal Son Penance

Adoration is the time chosen
for my penance as the prodigal son.
In the story, anyway, the father
runs to him, embraces him, kisses him.
No embrace for me.
The Father in sight seems a distant way
on the other side of the monstrance.
Just this wonderful (still)
"spiritual" sense of being loved. whoopee.
I want an embrace, hug from the Father
and ask for it, like your Son said, Lord,
a-s-k, ask seek knock. Nothing.
I am pissed.
Really pissed. And then I am very sad.
Later lying in bed, gut-wrenching tears.
Rejection from anyone else, Lord,
I can take it, but not from you.
Blurry eyes in the bed look out the window
and see in the trees the face of Jesus.
Earlier in the day watched for a long time
two pine branches of different trees
brushing against each other
the way playful lovers do with their hands.

In these trees I see this beautiful face of Jesus.
I ask a why? . . . We talk but he has no answer;
>	still, appreciate his presence.
Lord, this just reinforces old ways:
don't ask, don't seek, don't knock...
Can that be what you want?

So, went to bed pissed, woke up pissed,
and very sad.
Nope, not sad, just pissed. Staying with pissed
at you, Lord. Why do you want me angry?

A long day of the vulnerables.

You had to get me angry to get my attention.

> I want to be one with you.
> I want to know you.

>> Don't insist on me (your God)
>> entering your categories.
>> You, Steve, come into mine.

I want to be one with you in the way you want.

Then dusted off
another dusty retreat room cross.
They seem always dusty.

Come Holy Jesus

Come, Holy Jesus
Feed me with your life,
Savior and Brother and Friend;
Teach me your Way,
Forgive all my sin,
Jesus, come,
Holy Jesus, come.

(following Serafina di Giacomo's)

> Come, Holy Spirit
> Take hold of my life;
> Sign me with your holy love.
> Give me your gifts,
> Confirm me in faith,
> Spirit, come,
> Holy Spirit, come.

I Am Doing Something New

What new, Lord?
This how it seems:
your church disordered
and we're a good fit
for if my order corrected
as some would see fixed
'd be outgoing married
extrovert with twelve kids
instead of your celibate
priest hermit-wannabe
and "father" to so many.
What a funny joke.
I think I get it.

Bartimaeus,
to a Michael Jackson Melody?
(with sincere apologies to Jesus, Bartimaeus, Michael, and all)

REFRAIN:

> I want to walk in you, your way
> Leave my road-side-for-the Jesus way
> I want to walk in you, your way
> walk in Je-sus to-day.

Walkin' by now leav-ing Je-ri-cho
Who is that? Je-sus of Naz-a-reth!
Cryin' out, to "Son of Da-vid, King,
Show your mer-cy to me."

REFRAIN

"Shut your mouth,"
holl-ers the crowd a-round
He is just "too busy-for-a beg-gar blind,"
Cry-in' out to "Son of Da-vid, King,
Show your mer-cy to me."

REFRAIN

What'd they say?
Come now he's call-ing you
Say a-gain? Je-sus is call-ing you
Jump-ing up, throw-ing my stuff a-way,
"Show your mer-cy to me."

REFRAIN

"What d'you want   for me to do for you?"
"What I want,   Mas-ter is just to see"
"Go your way,   your faith is sa-ving you"
Showed his mer-cy to me.

REFRAIN

"I'm Barti-meus,   my eyes are o-pen free.
Was a beg-gar   cold blind, but now I see.
Je-sus, Mas-ter   gave to me faith and sight
and showed his mer-cy to me."

REFRAIN

(again, sincere apologies to all)

Labyrinth

Walking the labyrinth,
barefoot
a good hurt on recycled tire treads
like good reflexology,
feet that pleasant numb with shoes back on.

Walk the grounds around
to a big sacred heart cemetery statue
with a face that favors cousin saint Donnie,
handsome Jesus,
sensation of
walking in Jesus.

Resurrection Emotions

Matthew's two Marys fear and overjoy.
Mark's Marys and Salome tremble bewilder.
Luke's Marys and Joanna puzzle amazed fear.
John's Mary of Magdala weeps.
Matthew's eleven worship and doubt.
Mark's "companions" unbelieve.
Luke's Cleopas and companion are downcast
        astounded with hearts burning.
Luke's disciples are in startled terrified
        troubled incredulous amazed joy.
John's disciples are afraid and rejoice.
John's Thomas doubts all the way to
        "My Lord and My God."
John's seven go fish
        and dare not ask, "Who are you."
John's Peter is distressed.
Act's eleven gaze intently at the sky.
Act's crowd is confused astonished amazed
        astounded bewildered.
Mark's eleven preach everywhere.

A Take On That Oldest English Poem

Now we honor
heaven-guard
architect-might
and purpose:
Lord eternal
begins the wonders.
Holy creator
creates
heaven-roof
for the children.
Humanity-guard,
Lord eternal,
Lord almighty,
appoints
middle earth
land for humans.

A Real Desire

Lord, it was a real desire
gift of Ludwig and Joplin
but guessing not so strong
because "not now" meant
"that was it" almost as if
something in me was
pleased to have evidence
that it is a waste of time
to a-s-k, ask seek knock
and it wasn't a hero giving in
to needs more pressing
out of love of brothers.
It was, "Steve, you know
you're not worth it."
"It's a kick," temporary
anyway, it'll go away
well it did not go away
still middle-age teachable
at least by you, Lord.
So, just ask yourself,
is it still an honest desire?
And go from there.

Investigation

It wasn't that momma didn't hug me,
though there is no memory such,
but my wiring was to separate early
with ambivalence(?) to both momma
and deddy? Wonder what they
were thinking and feeling
as I sent those signals . . .
or were they so tired out as to be
relieved, or did they notice?
Did I hurt their thinkings and feelings?
Momma, Deddy, you can let me know.
Funny thing this Jesus thing:
to forgive and be forgiven
gonna have to forgive myself.

September 11 Morning

Memory of that
ninth month morning
coming to my safe office
after ordinary eucharist:
Mary walks in
with the radio news.
Barb turns on the tv
and begins the reporting.
Just went about my busy-
ness;
slowly did it sink in slowly.

The Children

Lord, it is the children
who suffer most for our sins
of dishonest pleasure seeking greed;
adults avoid pain and children suffer.
Lord, give grown-ups the grace strength
to look at our pain
and absorb it in holy honesty
and thus let your sons and daughters
grow in body, mind, soul and strength.
In this we need your help, Lord. Help!

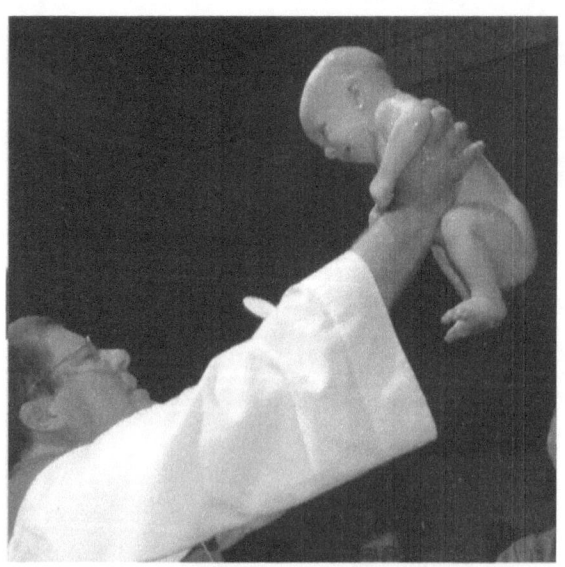

Free Slave

Your servant Paul, Lord,
called himself and your people
slaves.

Truth uncovers in being aware
of your grace that makes us
free.

So keep me chained, Lord, to you
grateful to be your
free slave

and loving being your brother.

Betty the Poet

Betty, the long-time housekeeper
without seeing me for a long time
sees me before a St. Ann funeral
and says what she sees:
    "Well look at you,
      you've gotten fat!
      You look gooood!"
She meant it as a compliment
so that's how I chose to take it.

Advent Silence

The silence
of a warm room on a cold day
squirrels and birds in the trees over the creek
@ work @ play, the praise of being a bird,
something to hear besides the stretch of sock
distraction: toenails that soon need a trim…
but something else is on true holy ground,
a sound of an animal not unlike a smoke alarm,
no not a machine noise, but more real
wait, is that a siren? someone in pain?
a quick sign of the cross,
our oddly resurrectional dance
which does not interrupt
either silence or nature noise
but lets me hear the icon eyes
of my Lord @ the window,
and get on back to those squirrels.

Morning Treasure

Missed two
early morning appointments
in one week,
thinking because
morning prayer time
is such a treasure;
but is it that it's time with you, Lord,
or just that it's time with no one else?
Honestly can't tell
but still trust
that you, Lord,
treasure it with me.

Gift from Little Grace

Little girl with the name of Grace
gave a picture gift.

"That's you (on the cross);
 that's the other Father (Mike);
 and that's God the Mother (on right)
 and that's my love for you (the heart)"

Thank you God for loving me
and thank you for the gift of Grace.

Poverty Immensity

Watching a poverty video
keeps me thinking
of an old friend in Haiti.
Gotta do something,
the dominating thinking.
Immensity Poverty
is the spacious place
of the incarnation.
Gotta do something
to help my friend
not to get a handle
or do a mere little
but as part of letting
you, Lord, take me
to the spacious place,
the one I can enter
only by your hand.
Bless all.

Evolution of a Hike-Breath Prayer

From the
Meinrad monk: Humility is reality;
pride is illusion.

First edit on
a long hike: Humility is reality;
pride is illusion;
lazy fear too: an illusion.

An edit of a
wise priest: Humility is reality;
pride is illusion;
laziness is a cop-out.

One
more: Humility is reality;
pride an illusion;
the lazy lie too, an illusion.

There is no place where God is not.

Before the Crucifix

Why, Beautiful Man,
do we treat you this way?
One answer comes:
a mumbled
embarrassed
thank you
that you transfigure
into holy gratitude grace.

Last Leaves

Those last leaves still clinging
with a shape looking alive but airlight
how long, Lord, can they stay in their dance
of bird pretense in the tree limb end where
a squirrel won't bother, as if there would ever
be a reason for a squirrel to chase a leaf
falling featherly, but then who cares?
So there you are, leaf with neighbor leaves,
waiting in your chilly dance for the sun ray,
perhaps knowing that snow is on the way and
if that doesn't do the job there will be
the inevitable tennessee ice storm, and surely
that will bring you to the ground.

When that ice is melted by spring rising
we will sing alleluia, but before that
we will feel the ash warning and before that
we will shout ho ho ho, and still before that
we wait in the advent with leaves still clinging.

Christmas Eve

Meeting, greeting, eating, drinking, joking,
sitting, standing, chatting chit heart to heart,
joy of another year of the grow-die change,
standing between Christmas Eve masses
meeting and greeting
first the goers and then the comers,
a little boy dressed up in round eye excitement
gives a hug and a greeting and explodes:
 "I am five!"
My chit-chat, "Five is a good age,"
 prompts a question, "Were you five?"
and I put my hand in blessing on
 his thick black hair to give my pitch:
 "There was a day when I was
  exactly as tall as you are right now."
 and his smile is about to catch fire.
Going in to seal the deal, bending down
 with an eye to mom and dad:
 "There was a day when Jesus was
  exactly as tall as you are right now."
A pondering wonder
stretching out of those five years,
he turns out his proclamation: "Cooooolllll!"

A Dream

A dream so full of sex and violence
the desire to wake was overcome only by
the desire to stay in the story,
winding up landing down in and out
of the comfortable excitement of a gang,
belonging to each, faithful to one,
the risk of bad timing and the joy
of the lucky choice and fruit of faith,
it's a dream: it's not supposed to make sense,
so waking up brings a sad gratitude that while
dream memory is no more real than yesterday
neither can compete with life still waiting
for a boring day.
Take a leak, wash your face, clean your teeth,
brush your hair, put on some real clothes
and sit down with coffee and a psalmbook.
And later on, call that old friend in the dream.

Lord, What You Up To Today?

Leaves now in the bushes none yet on the trees
but buds beginning;
a fight-gang forming or a team for play?
Transition in process, nothing else… Just wait.
But it's never nothing else;
there's always something more.
Lord, what you up to today?

See now the cloud-sky gray with a blue-hint;
stare at the tree limbs long enough and see
the buds are greening!
In these summer nights to come when
cloudless we will sit still long enough to see
more and more stars and more and more.
Just by looking! Can't wait!
Lord, what you up to today?

Ezekiel Song

REFRAIN: You are our God\,
          your peo-ple are we, A-le-lu-ia!

Lord God/, Sab-a-oth, El, A-do-nai,
Proph-et E-ze-ki-el's song we lift high:
Spir-it and heart\, re-newed you pro-vide,
    You are our God...
REFRAIN

Take us out-side all the pride that div-ides,
Gath-er us in from the coun\-tries wide,
Bring us back in-to your land at your side,
    You are our God...
REFRAIN

Sprin-kle on us\ your wa\-ters clean,
From our im-pur-it-ies make us to wean,
Clean from i-dol-a-try let us be seen,
    You are our God...
REFRAIN

Take from the flesh\ the hearts\ of stone,
Re-new with hearts\ that beat to your tone,
In-to the bod-y your Spir-it be shown,
    You are our God...
REFRAIN

Text: Ezekiel 36:24-28
Music: 888, O FILII ET FILIAE, Chant Mode II, *Airs sur les hymnes sacrez*, 1623
Popular melody for *Ye Sons and Daughters Let Us Sing*

Beach Ministry

Seagulls stand in the wind
and seem to call complaint
about the lazy priest on a
vacation chair, cooler beside,
on hot sand under umbrella
so burning sun shielded
and enjoyed under good breeze.
Little girls play their games
and birds and priest
mind their own happy business.

What is Faith?

In the seminary and taking a course
called "Fundamental Theology;"
there was a problem: not getting it.
Not fundamental enough?
Too essential?
Couldn't seem to get it.
Off to the teacher, a brilliant man
who rubbed his baldness and beard
and silenced me with a question:
So tell me; what is faith?
No response came because
there was no answer in me.
How could such a smart man
ask such a stupid question?
Faith just is, like hope, like love,
it just is. And my only answer
left me stupid: Faith is faith.
The teacher rubbed his baldness
and beard and smiled, and
I felt impossibly more stupid.
Years later now, it could be worse;
could have come to an answer
instead of an alleluia.

Again Again

boy in off-balance tilt
hot sun beyond flight
above cool water
below daddy's catch
and for all to hear:
"again! again!"

Miracle Of Now

In all ways ordinary
is the miracle of now
I want to watch on news cast
but nothing new about it
so art alone reports it
yet its could be the telling
that washes trivia clear
from all true seeker-eyes
and opens wide real hunger
for beauty-goodness-truth
still resting in the waiting
for the always ordinary
in the miracle of now.

inspired by words of Katherine Vaz

...the ordinary miracle of saying *this, now, with you*, this suffices me.

in "Baptism"
in *Signatures of Grace: Catholic Writers on the Sacraments*,
edited by Thomas Grady and Paula Huston,
published by Dutton, a division of Penguin Putman Inc.
New York. Copyright 2000 by Katherine Vaz

Good Guy

I tried to be a good guy
and put out some seed for the birds
but this one dang squirrel climbed
and rocked it out for all its own
so birds came to the unfed feeder
accusing me, the café proprietor.

I'm not in it for the money!
If the squirrel cannot obey the rules
then seed stays stored dry in the tin.
If birds go hungry it's not my fault.
Just trying to be a good guy, I've become
just one more dang fat hoarding squirrel.

Turtle Walk

Watched today this turtle
step down a slope to the water
mostly like this:
six awkward steps and a rest,
six awkward steps and a rest,
one time five, another time seven,
most often six (pokes? strides?
lurches? twists? lift-up-fall-downs?
I'll call 'em steps) and then a rest,
same pace from below the tree,
down the grass, over through mud,
and into the water
where no accountants are watching.

Blessed Are

Bless-ed are you in spir-it poor
you bless-ed in true pov-er-ty:
to-tal de-pend-ence on the Lord;
yours is the king-dom of your God.

Too bless-ed now are you who mourn
and weep the tears of hu-man grief;
let go the hurt and a-ny sin,
be com-fort-ed and laugh a-gain.

Bless-ed are you who with the meek
em-brace the risk to fol-low Christ;
mind, bod-y, soul, in will-ing strength,
in-her-it too your land of rest.

You bless-ed hun-gry, you who thirst:
your thirst and hun-ger sat-is-fied
in right-eous-ness, in jus-tice due,
our source of joy and grat-i-tude.

And bless-ed you who mer-cy show,
re-ceived in mea-sure giv-en well:
the great-est gift of Je-sus Christ,
so wise are you who claim this prize

Bless-ed are you, the clean of heart,
in sing-le fo-cus on the good
who live in free-dom blem-ish free,
your cen-ter, God, whom you shall see.

And bless-ed you who make the peace
be-yond what hu-mans un-der-stand
in pa-tient prayer and lis-ten-ing,
called sons and daugh-ters of the King.

Re-joice in glad-ness, last-ing joy,
who for the sake of right-eous-ness
bear per-se-cu-tions for the good,
yours is the king-dom of our God.

Music: 8888 CONDITOR ALME SIDERUM
Popular melody for: *Creator of the Stars of Night*

Duck Dunner

Ducks have found a nest of something
and are taking their dunner.
No, Wolf, you're not yet hungry.
It's not time to take signals from a duck.
Would you look at that bird!
Put down your pencil
and let God's creatures
write their own poem.

Night-long Rain

Night-long rain has sunk the algae
and the lake looks cleaner
but is it an illusion of dilution?
Hard to say, but the ducks
swim more freely and lovebirds
fly lower their reflected song
and why do I care? Well,
since it's all about me, it's time
to shower the algae off my
smelly body with a morning rain.
Thank you, Lord,
for that night-long rain.

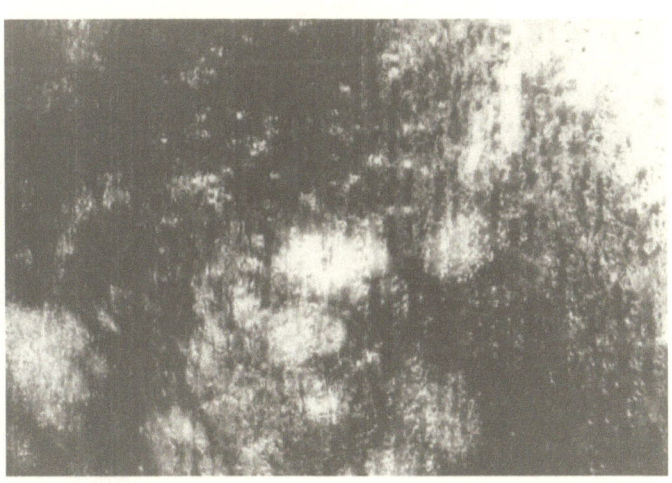

A Te Deum Rendering

O God,
  we praise you and know you as Lord.
Father everlasting,
  all of the earth does worship you.
To you all angels cry aloud,
  the heavens, all powers,
  and cherubim and seraphim continually:
Holy, Holy, Holy, Lord God Sabaoth;
  heaven and earth are filled to the full
  with the majesty of your glory.
The glorious company of Apostles praise you;
in good gathering the Prophets praise you;
the noble testimony of Martyrs praise you;
the holy Church all over the world
knows you:
  our Father,
    in majesty infinite,
  your true
    and only Son,
  and Holy Spirit
    Comforter.

You, Christ, are the King of glory
  and everlasting Son of the Father.
Taking it onto yourself to deliver humanity
  you did not avoid the virgin womb.
Overcoming the sharp death you opened
  the kingdom of heaven to all believers.
You sit at the right hand of God
  in the glory of the Father.
And we believe you will come
  to be our judge.

Day by day in every place we give you thanks
  and ever praise your name.

Help your servants redeemed by your blood;
  number them with the saints in eternal glory.
Save your people and bless your heritage;
  govern us, Lord, and lift us to forever.
Keep us this day, Lord, without sin.
  Have mercy on us, Lord, have mercy;
  let your mercy rest upon us.

And give to me, Lord, the grace to be aware
  of humble dignity in holy honesty.
In you, Lord, is my trust.

www.ingramcontent.com/pod-product-compliance
Lightning Source LLC
Chambersburg PA
CBHW030330080526
44584CB00012B/792